W9-CFQ-564

Spot the Difference

Wings

Diyan Leake

Heinemann Library
Chicago, Illinois

Customer Service 888-454-2279
Visit our website at www.heinemannraintree.com

Designed by Joanna Hinton-Malivoire
Printed in China by South China Printing Company Limited

12 11 10 09 08
10 9 8 7 6 5 4 3 2 1

ISBN-10: 1-4329-0003-X (hc)
ISBN-10: 1-4329-0008-0 (pb)

The Library of Congress has cataloged the first edition as follows:
Leake, Diyan.
  Wings / Diyan Leake. -- 1st ed.
      p. cm. -- (Spot the difference)
  Includes bibliographical references and index.
  ISBN 978-1-4329-0003-8 (hc) -- ISBN 978-1-4329-0008-3 (pb)
  1. Wings--Juvenile literature. I. Title.
  QL950.8.L43 2007
  591.47'9--dc22
                                        2007010531

Acknowledgments
The publisher would like to thank the following for permission to reproduce photographs: Corbis p. **20**; Creatas pp. **13**, **23** middle, **back cover**; FLPA/Minden Pictures/Tom Velo p. **15**; Getty Images/National Geographic p. **14**; Nature Picture Library pp. **18**, **4** (Kim Taylor), **7** (Hanne & Jens Eriksen), **8** (Tom Mangelsen), **12** (Kim Taylor); Photolibrary pp. **5** (Richard Packwood), **6** (John Downer), **9** (Tony Tilford), **10** (Tui de Roy), **17** (Tobias Bernhard), **22** (Tobias Bernhard), **23** bottom (Tui de Roy); Photolibrary/ Animals Animals/Earth Scenes p. **16**; Photolibrary.Com (Australia)/Geoff Higgins pp. **19**, **23** top; Photolibrary/Picture Press pp. **11**, **22**; Photolibrary/Workbook, Inc. p. **21**.

Cover photograph of a bald eagle reproduced with permission of Alamy (Steve Bloom).

Every effort has been made to contact copyright holders of any material reproduced in this book. Any omissions will be rectified in subsequent printings if notice is given to the publisher.

Contents

What Are Wings? 4

Why Do Animals Have Wings?. 8

Different Wings. 8

Amazing Wings. 14

Do People Have Wings? 20

Spot the Difference! 23

Index 24

What Are Wings?

Wings are part of a body.
Some animals have wings.

Wings are on the sides of the body.

Why Do Animals Have Wings?

Most animals use their wings to fly.

Some animals with wings cannot fly.

Different Wings

Wings come in many shapes.
Wings come in many sizes.

This is a bat.

It has thin wings.

wingspan

This is an albatross.

It has long wings.

This is a bee.
It has short wings

This is a ladybug.
It has small wings.

This is a dragonfly.
It has four wings.

Amazing Wings

This is a vulture.

It can fly very high.

This is a falcon.
It can fly very fast.

This is a hummingbird.
Its wings move very fast.

This is a penguin.
Its wings help it swim.

This is a butterfly.
Its wings have bright colors.

This is a cormorant.
Its wings dry in the sun.

Do People Have Wings?

People do not have wings.

People have feet and arms.

People can use their arms to move.

Spot the Difference!

Which animal uses its wings to swim?

Picture Glossary

 **cormorant** large, black sea bird

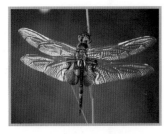 **dragonfly** long, thin insect with four wings

 **wingspan** length of a bird's wings when they are stretched out

Index

albatross, 10

bat, 9

bee, 11

butterfly, 18

cormorant, 19, 23

dragonfly, 13, 23

falcon, 15

hummingbird, 16

ladybug, 12

penguin, 17

people, 20, 21

vulture, 14

Note to Parents and Teachers

Before reading

Talk to the children about animals with wings. Have they seen birds flap their wings and fly? Talk about animals that have wings but which are not birds (such as bats, insects). What makes a bird special is that its wings are made of feathers. Talk about animals that have wings but do not fly (such as penguins, ostriches, emus, or kiwis).

After reading

- Hold a feather in your hand and stick your hand up as high as you can in the air. Let the feather float down to the floor. Talk to the children about how the feather is light and the air supports it. Explain how birds use the feathers on their wings to support them. Drop a ball from the same height and compare how it falls to the floor.
- Draw an outline of a bird and ask the children to stick feathers on it. Talk about putting the smaller feathers on the body and the longer feathers on the wings. Explain how to place the feathers in the same direction.